Frogs

Coloring Book

Delightful & Decorative Collection!
Patterns of Frogs & Toads For Adults & Children

Rachel Mintz

Images used under license from Shutterstock.com

Copyright © 2018 Palm Tree Publishing - All rights reserved.
No part of this publication may be reproduced, distributed, or transmitted in any form or by any means, including photocopying, recording, or other electronic or mechanical methods, without the prior written permission of the publisher, except in the case of brief quotations embodied in critical reviews and certain other noncommercial uses permitted by copyright law.

Join Our Coloring Books VIP Group
Members Get Giveaways, Deep Discount Offers,
Win Prizes – Visit Site To Join (It's Free)

www.ColoringBookHome.com

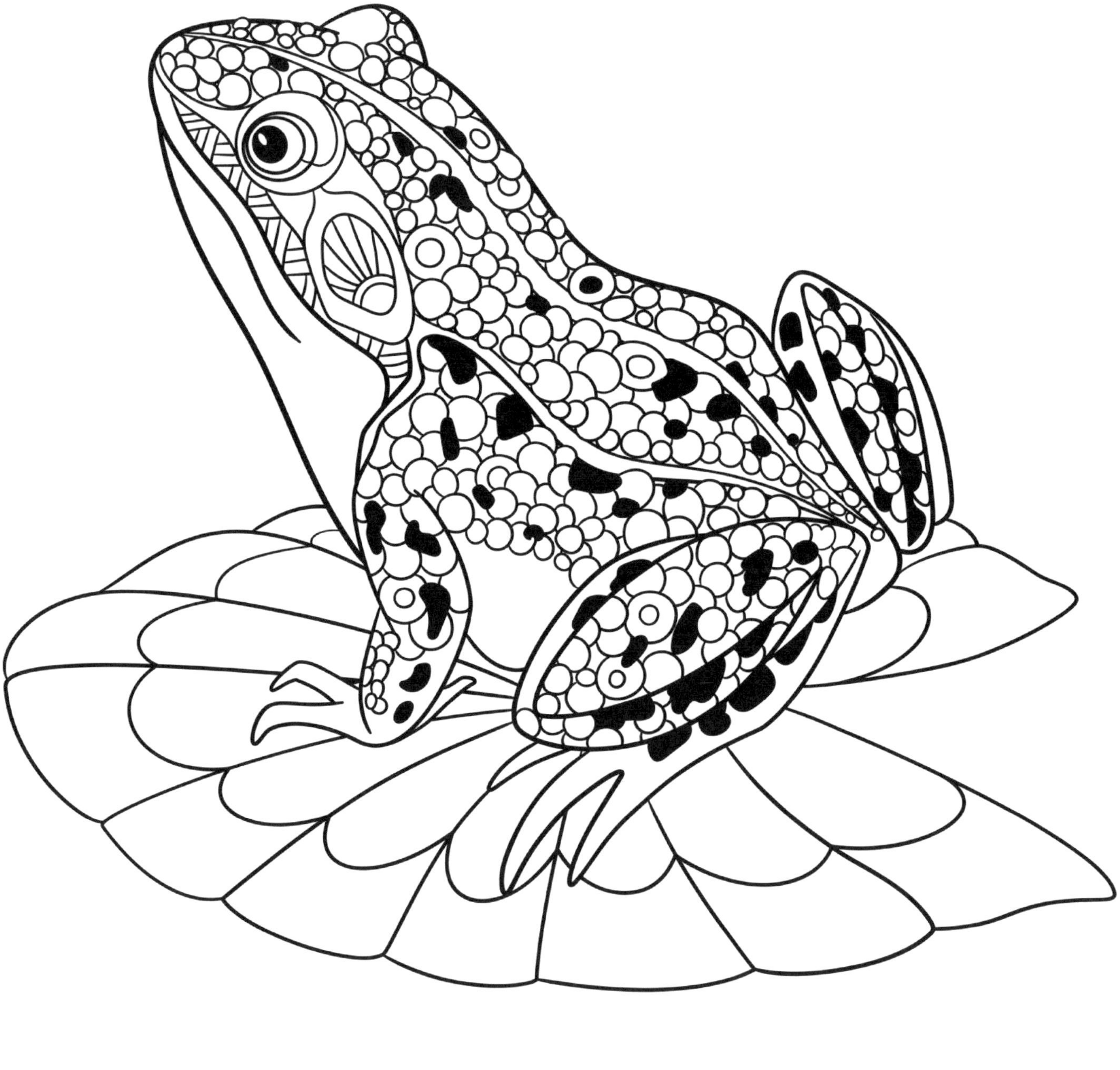

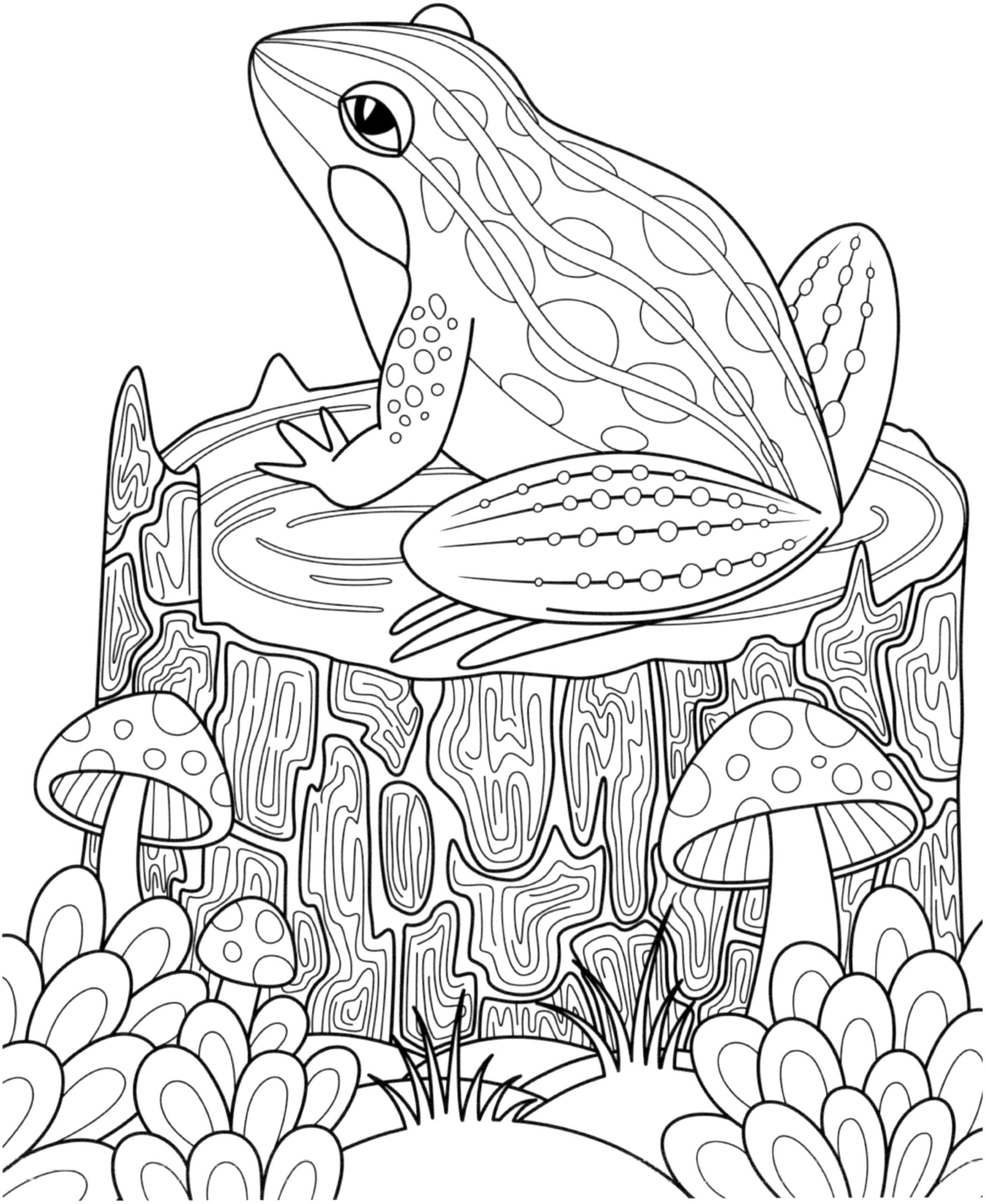

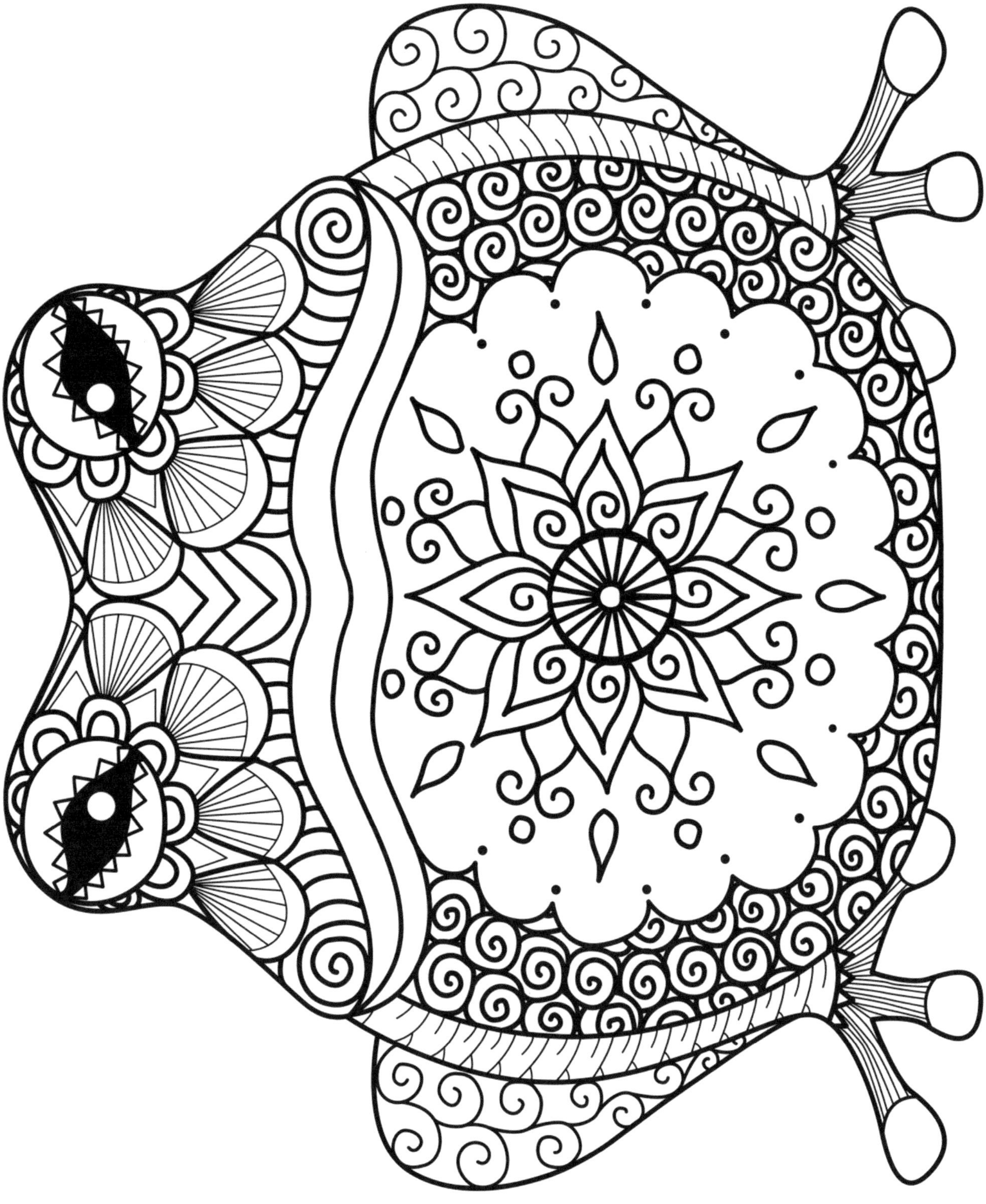

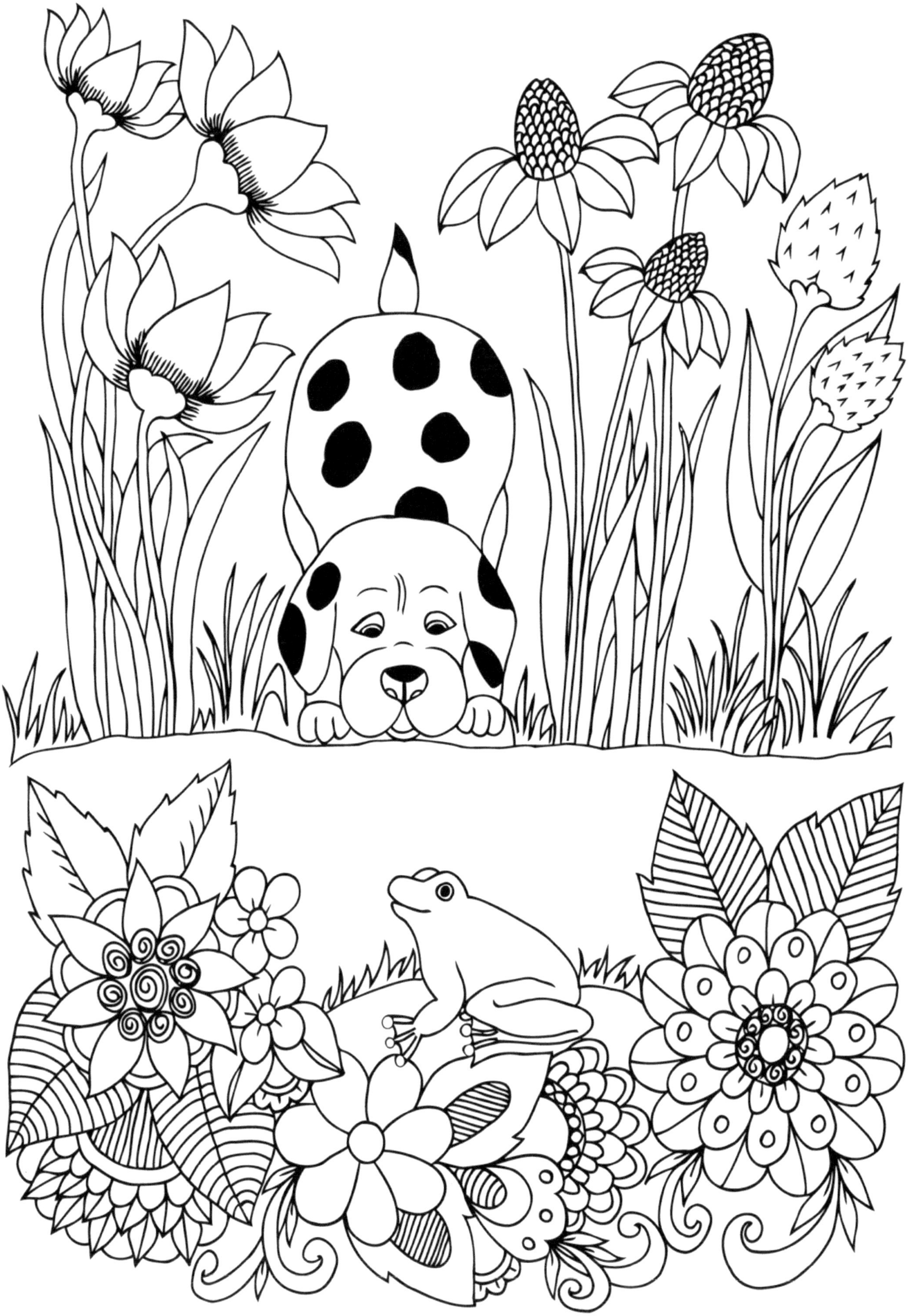

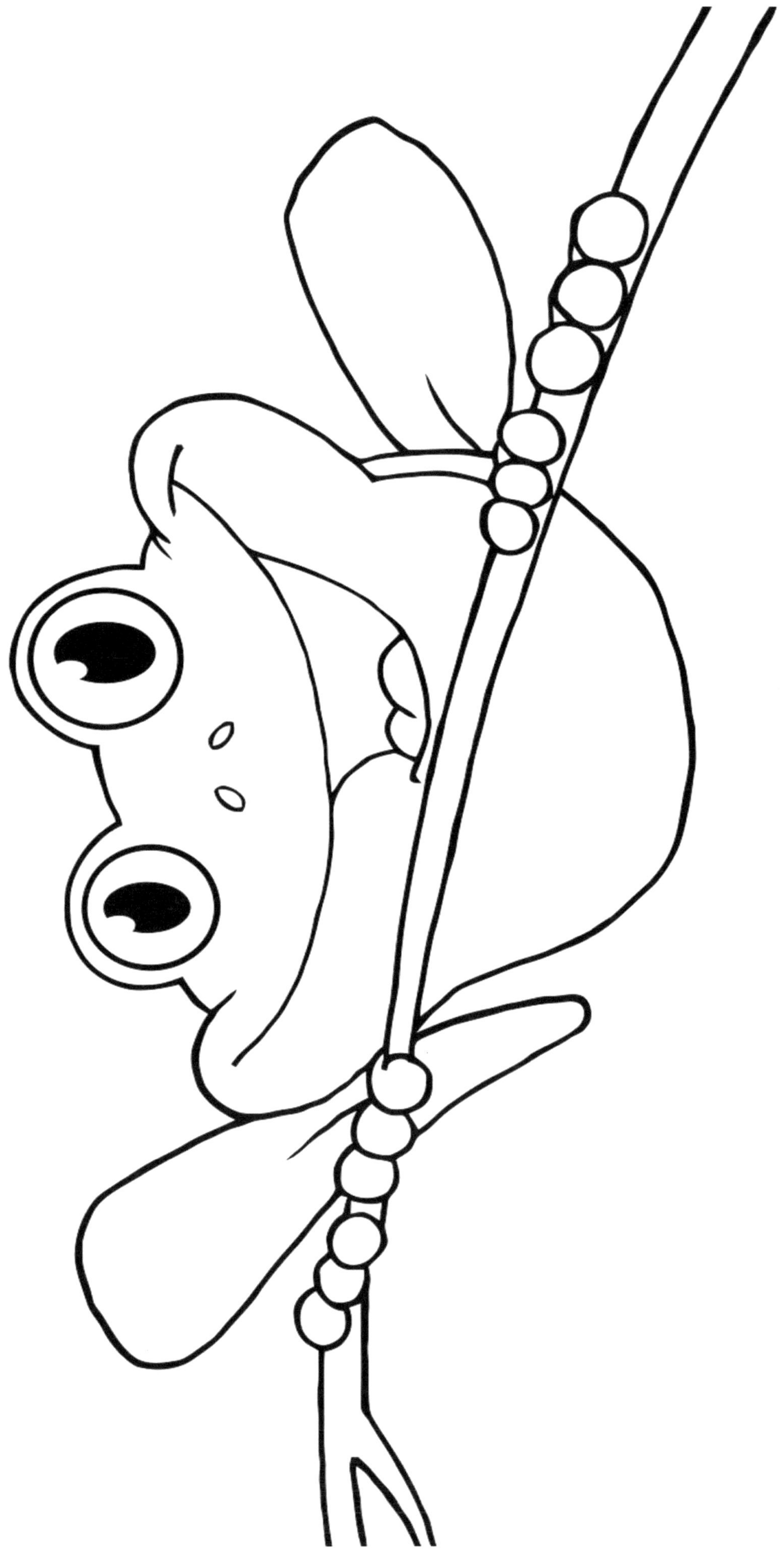

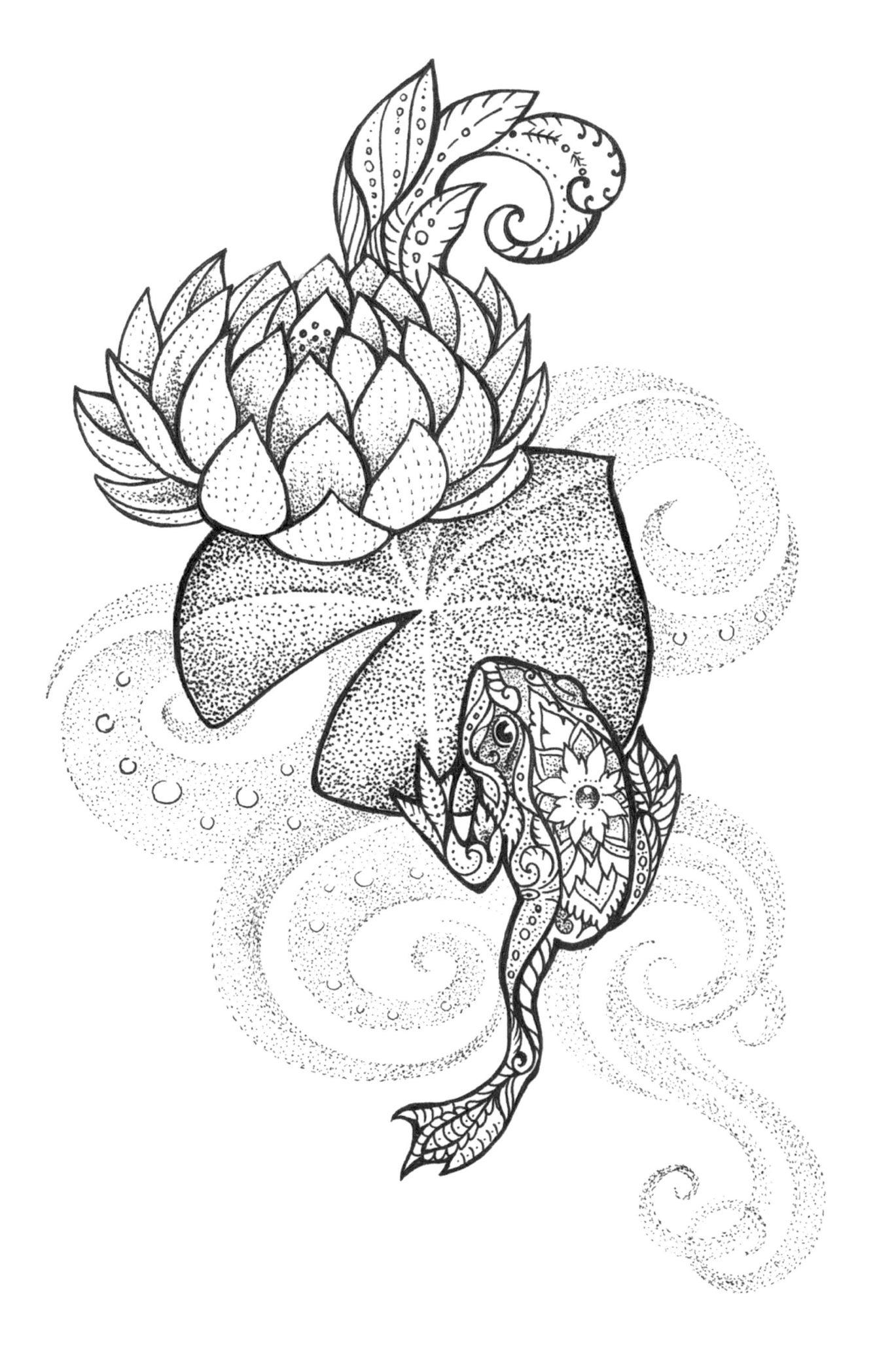

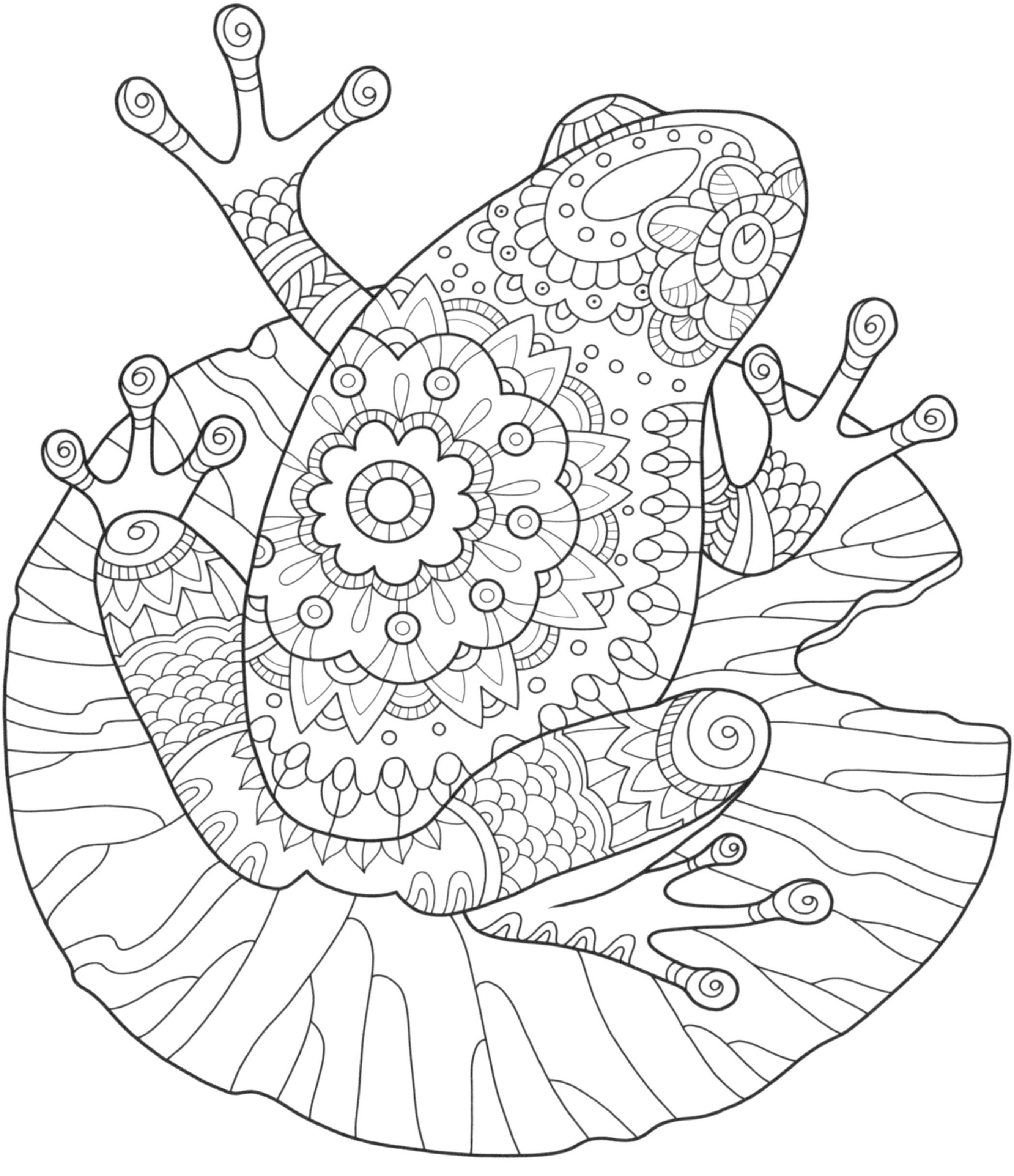

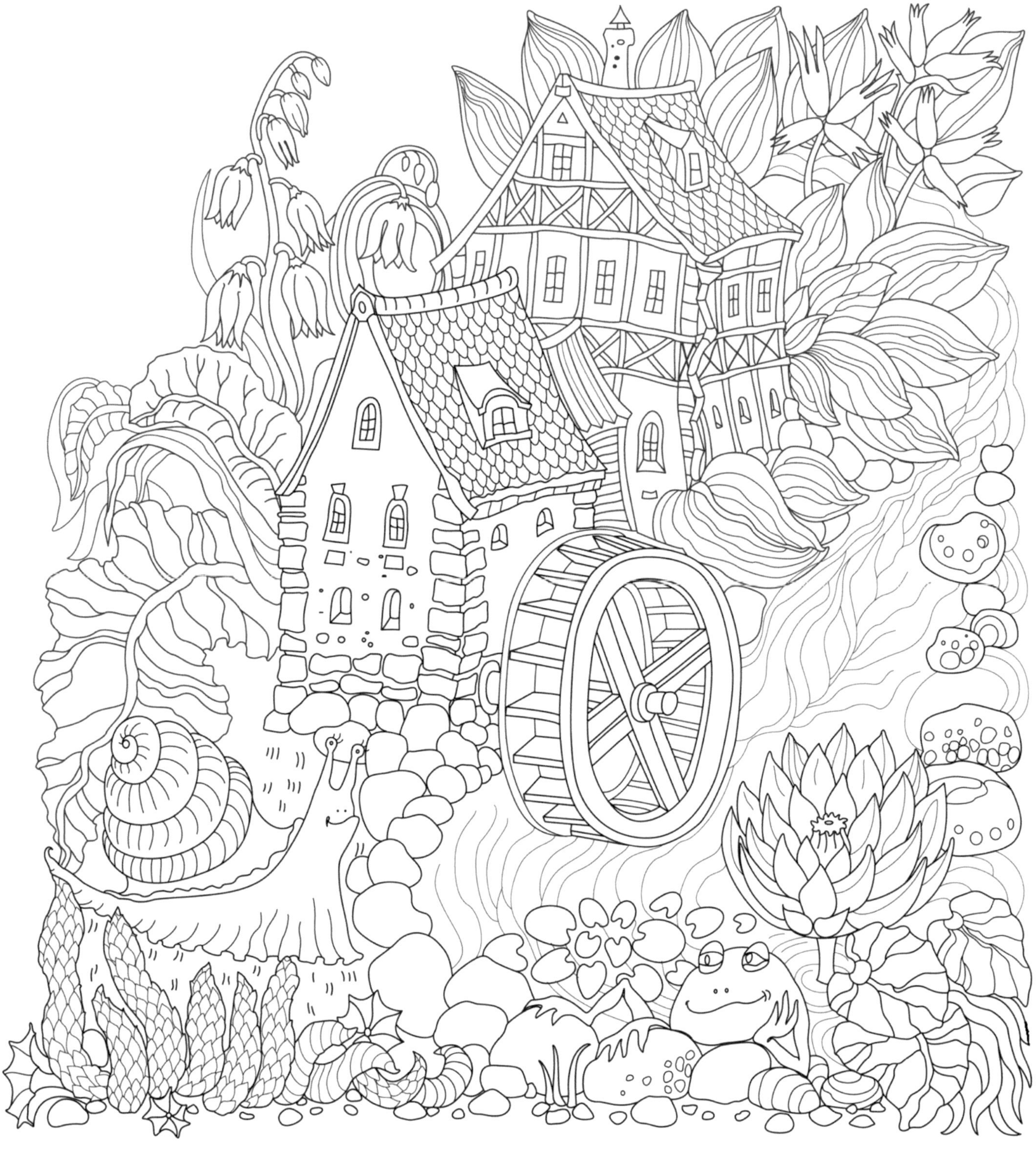

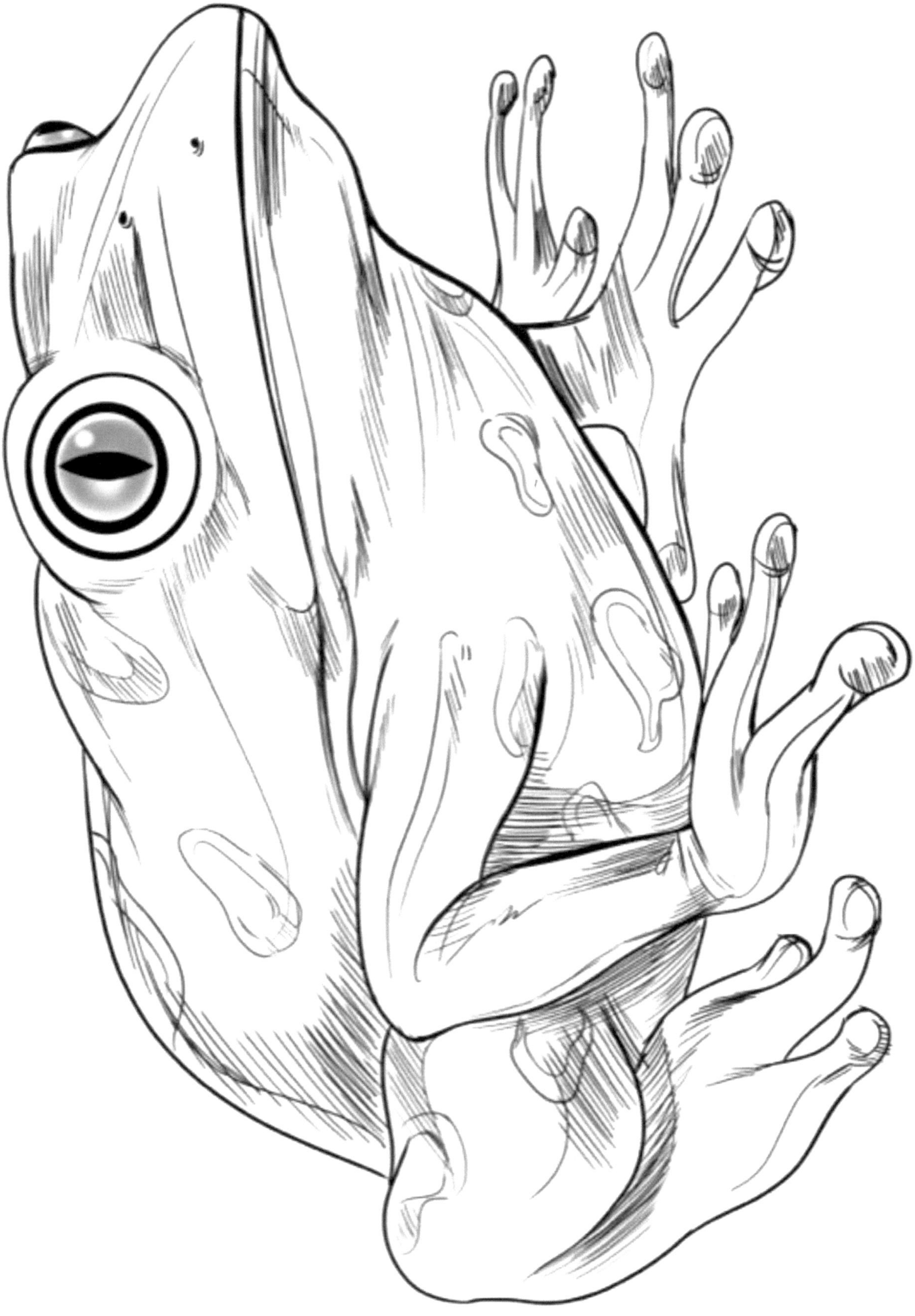

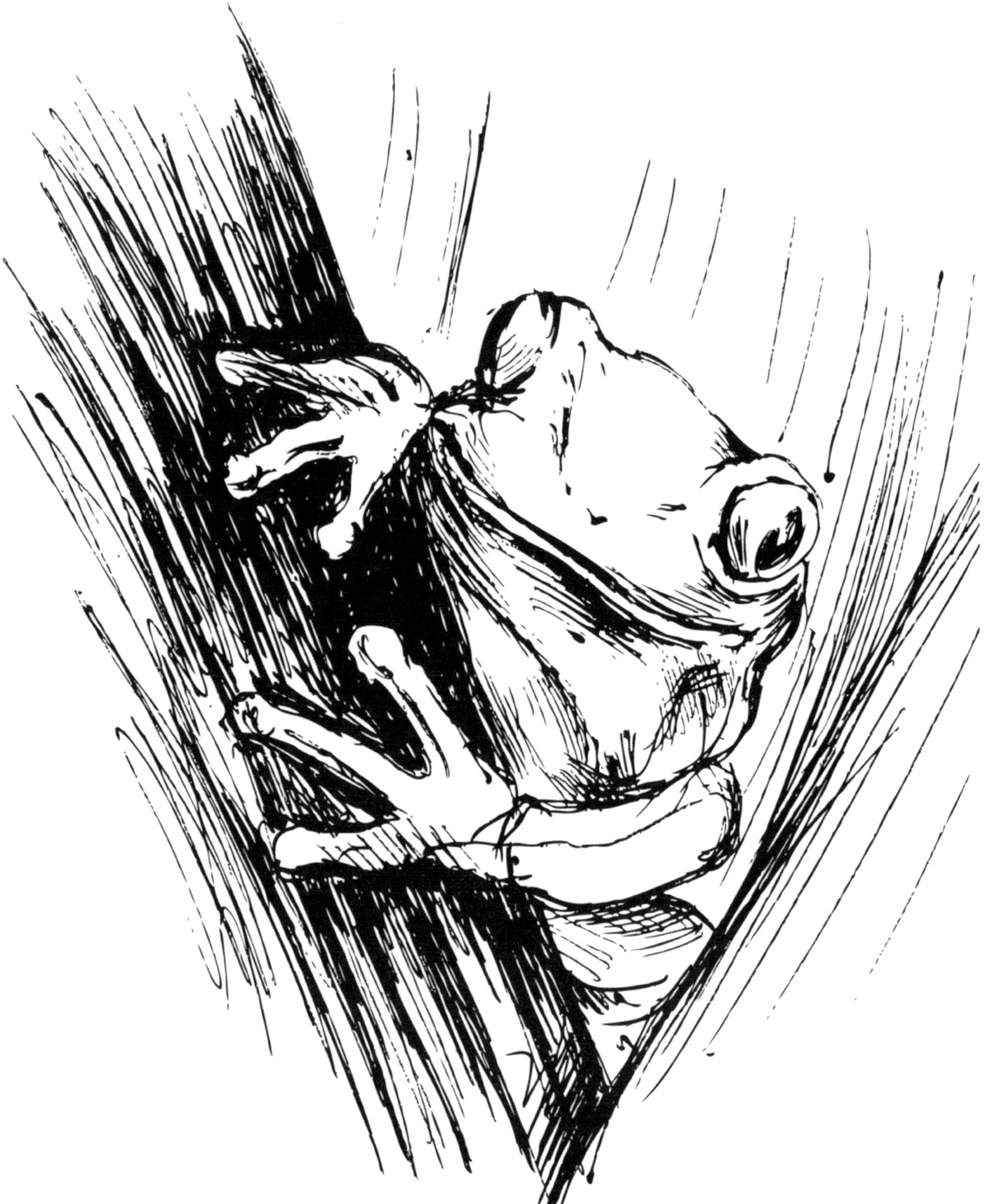

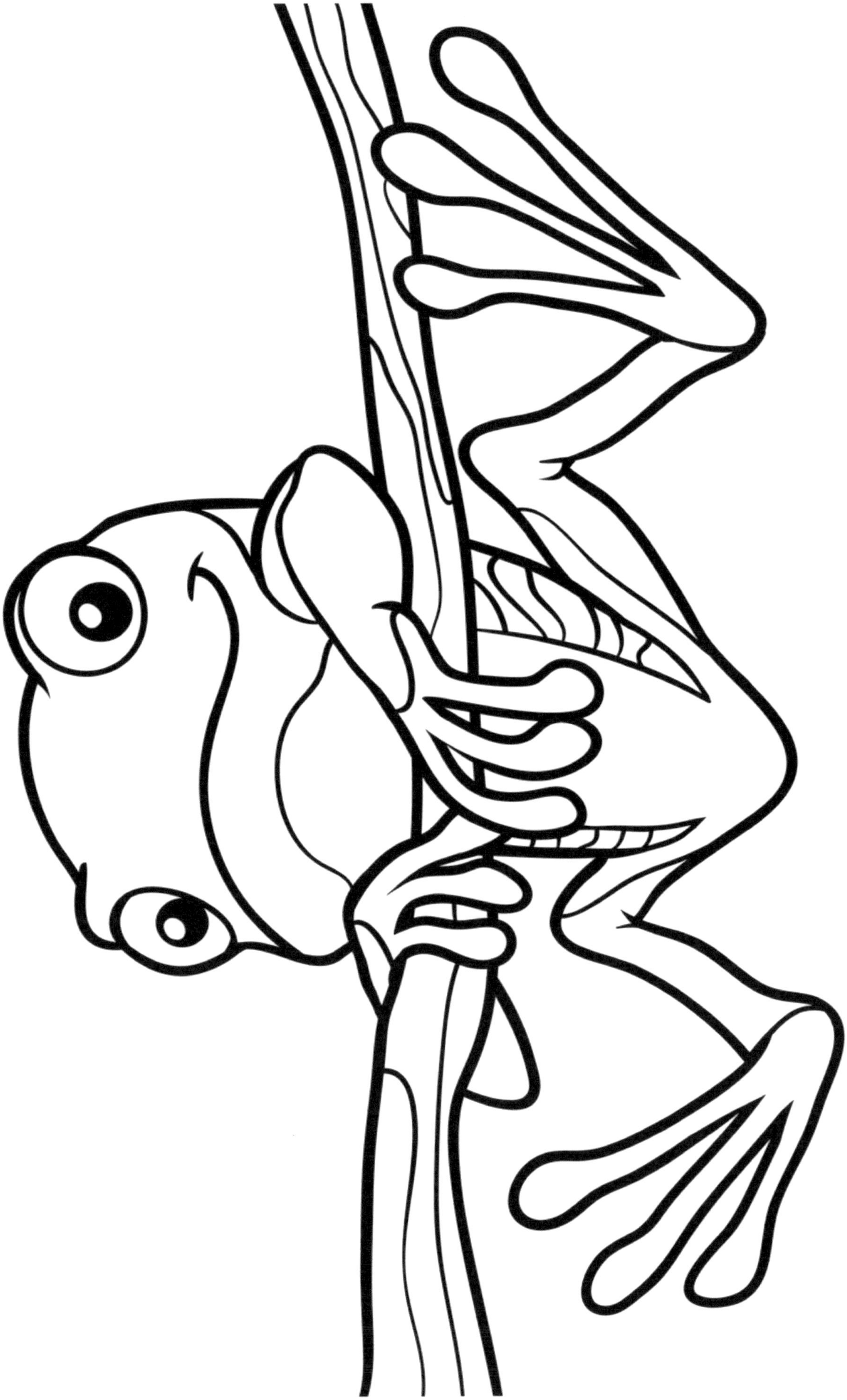

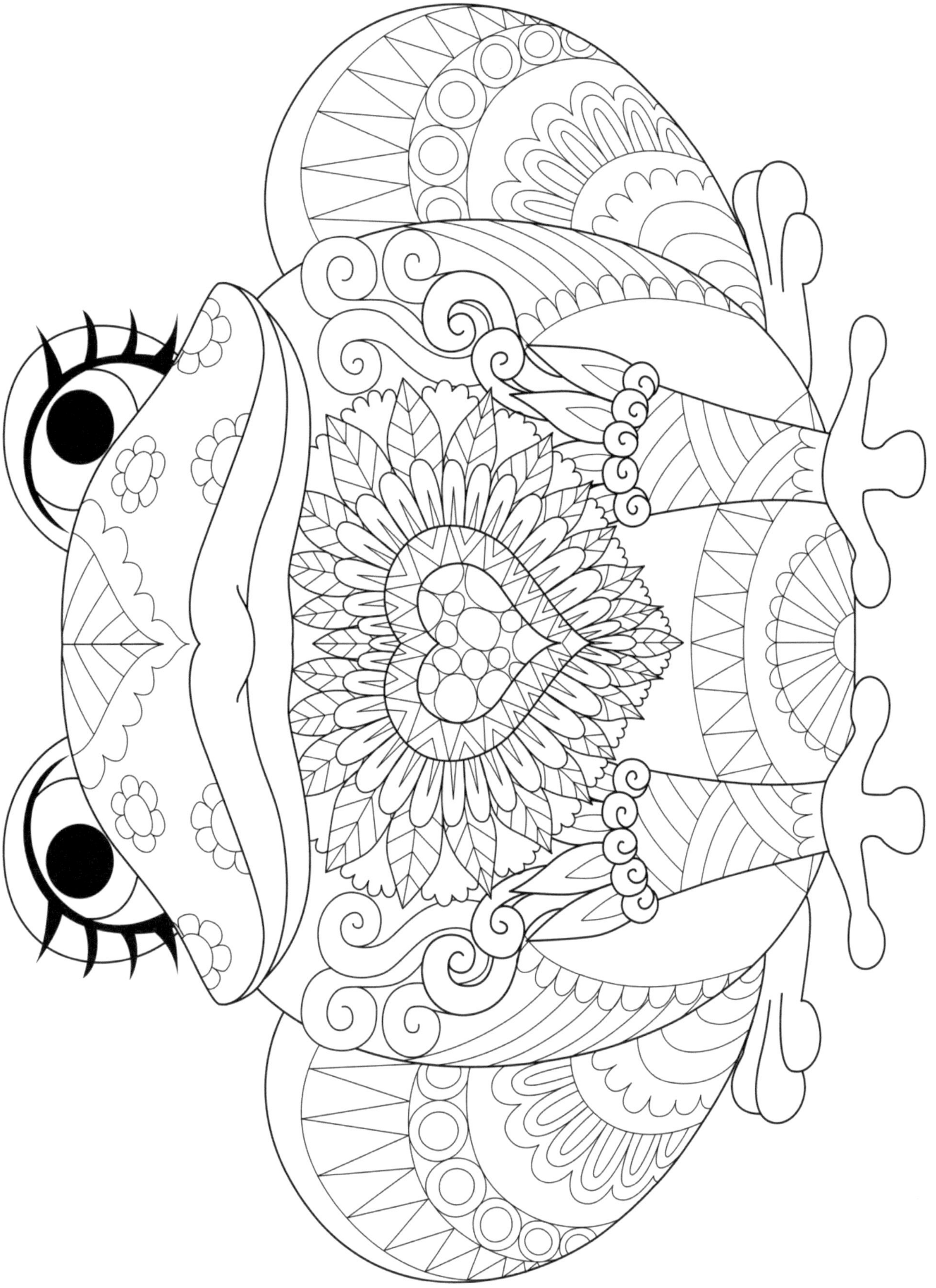

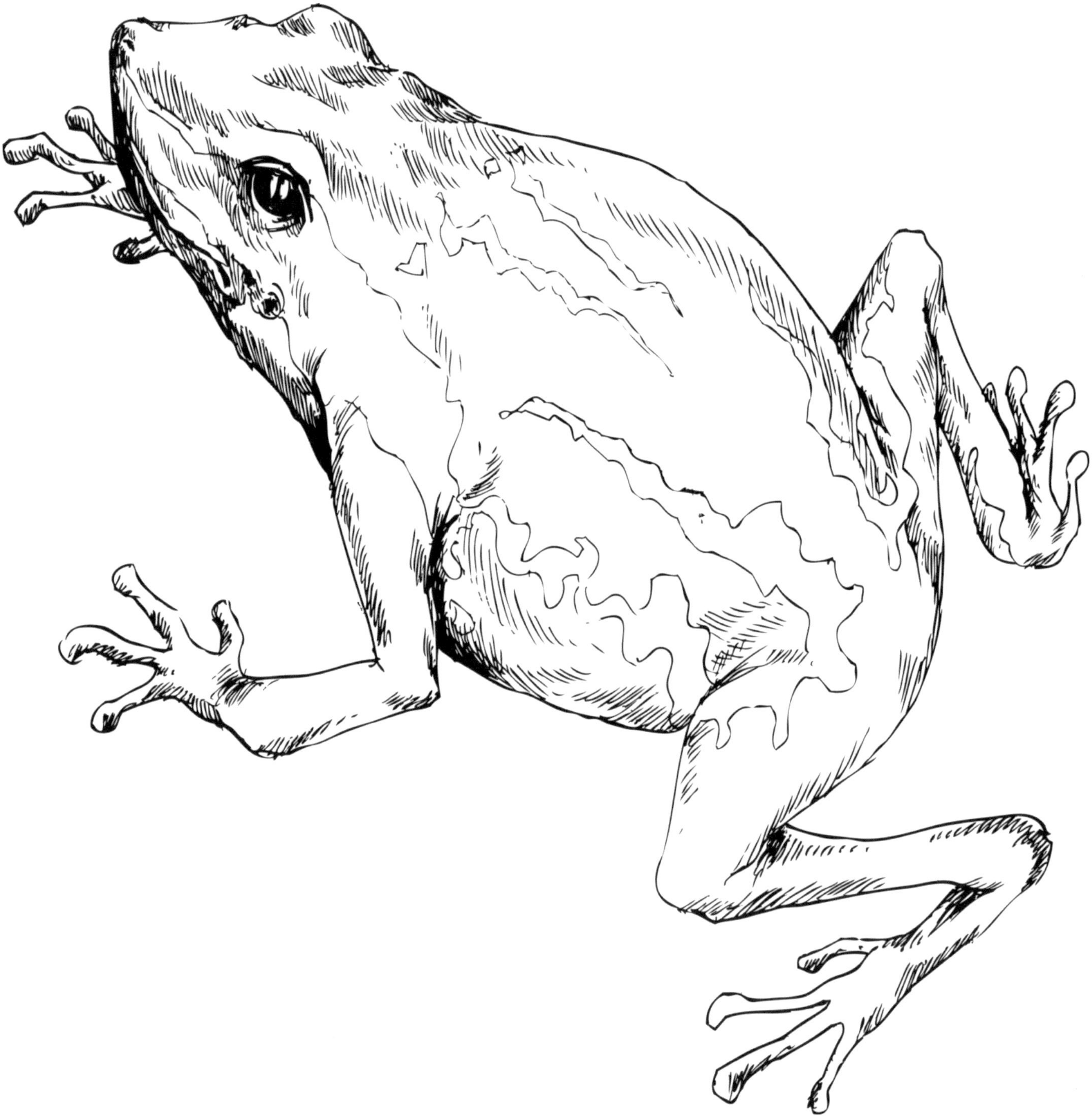

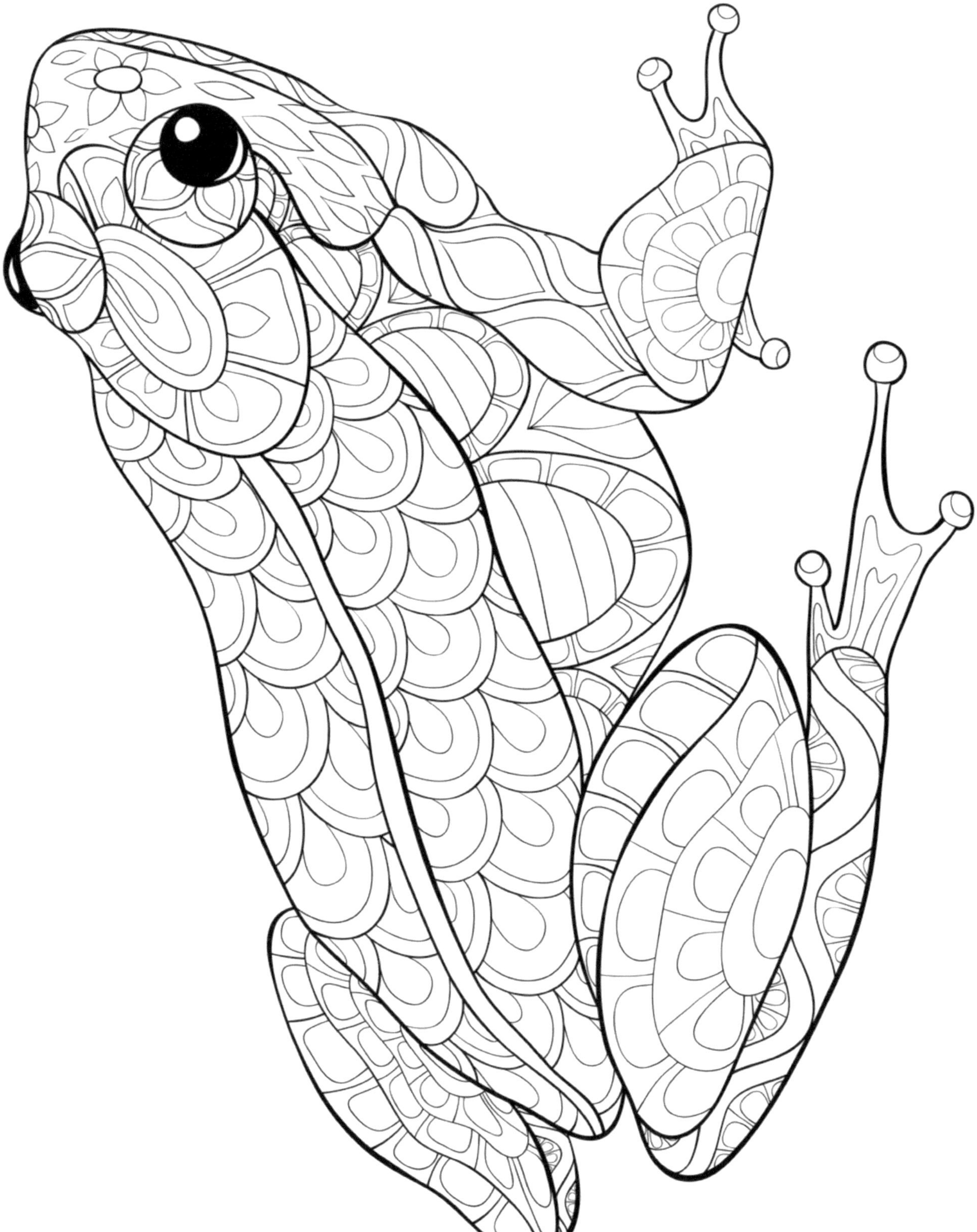

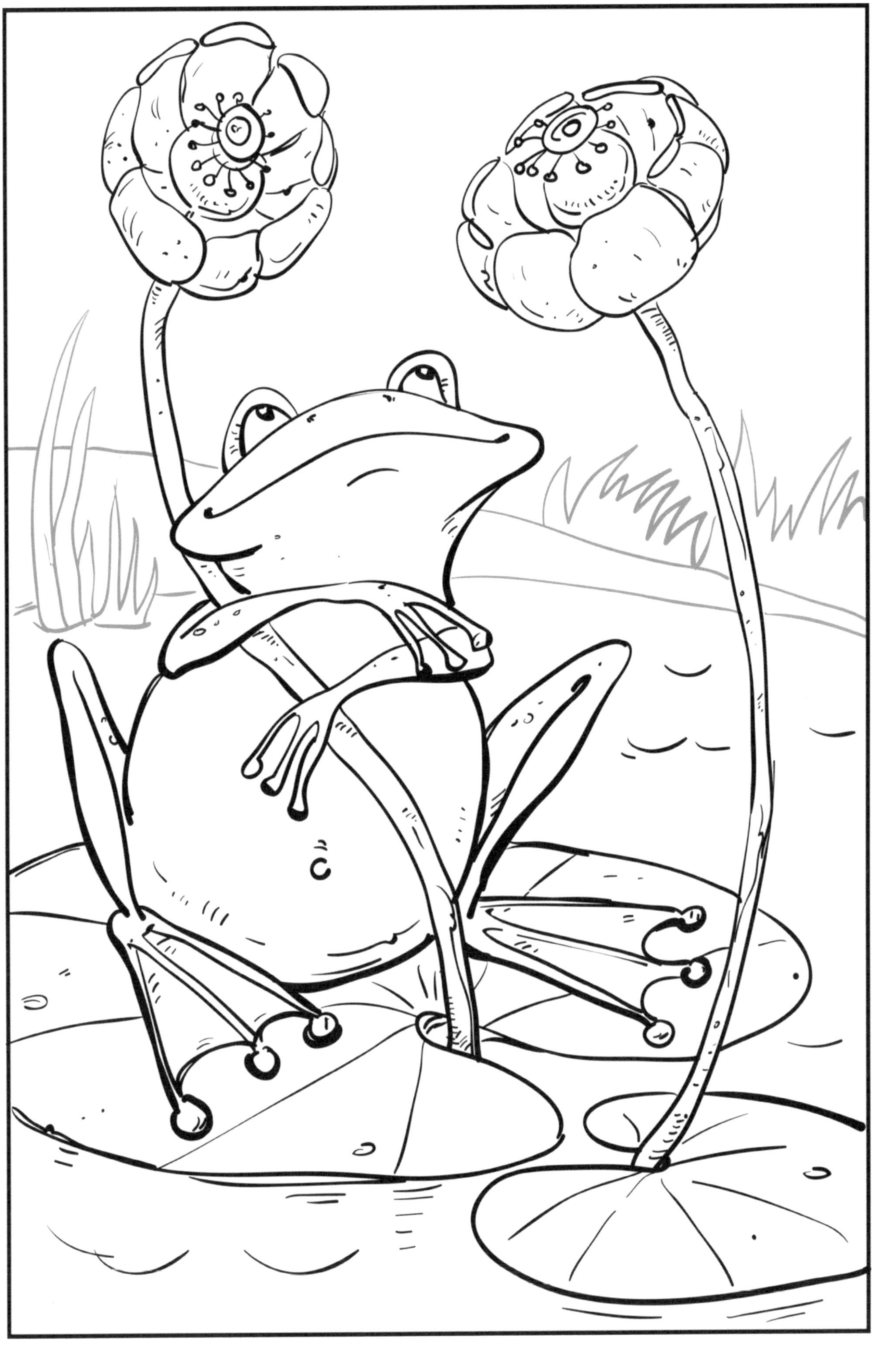

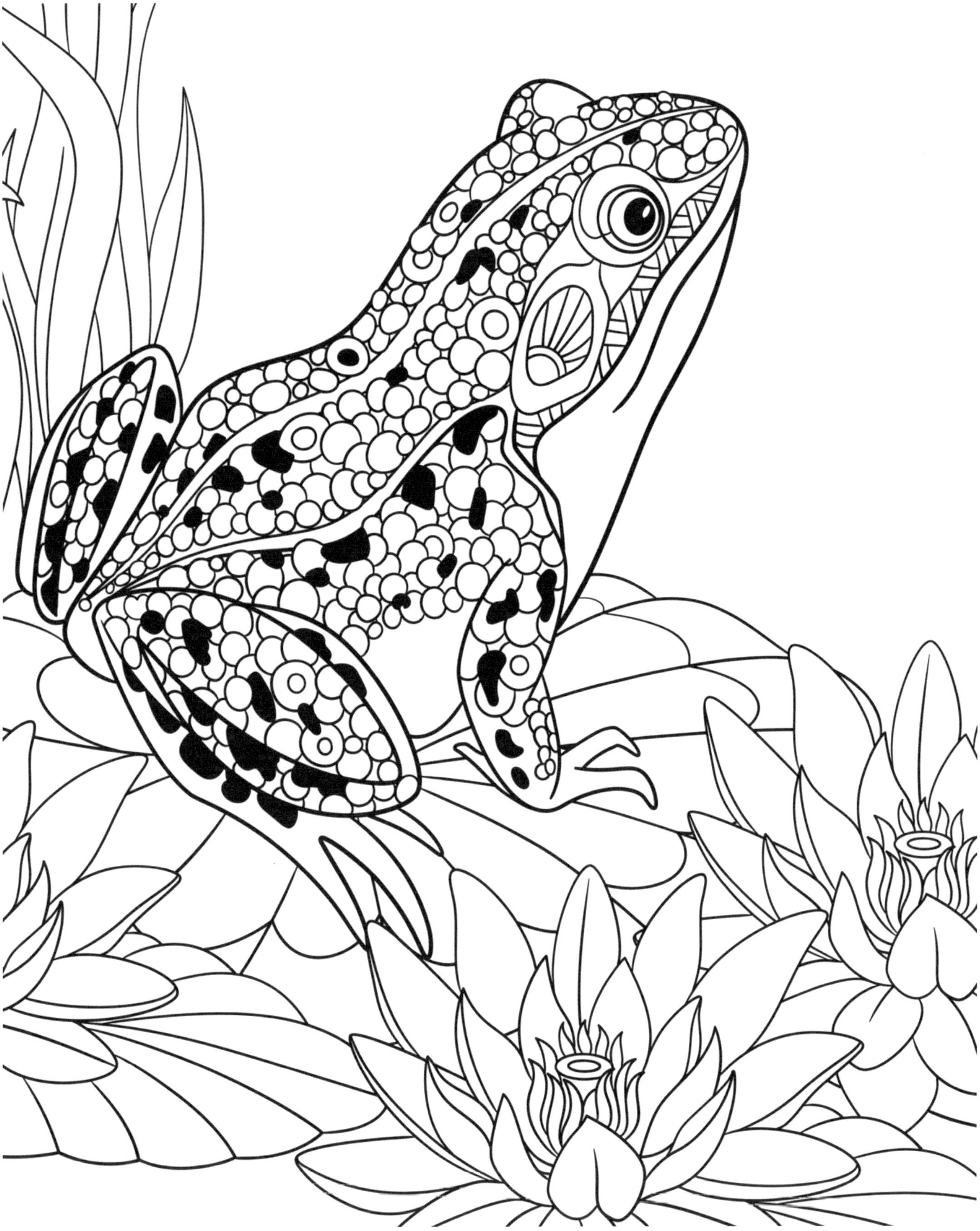

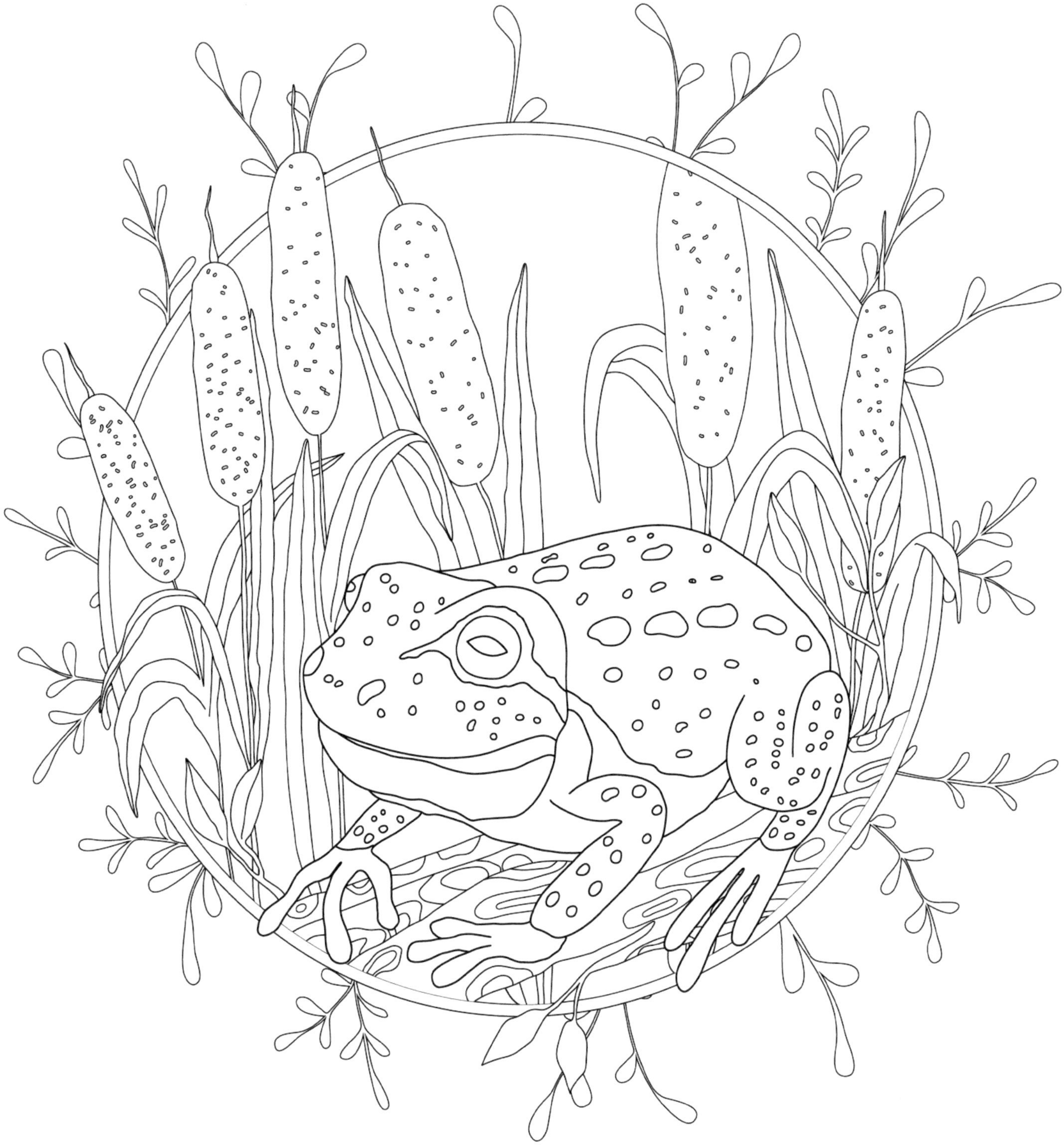

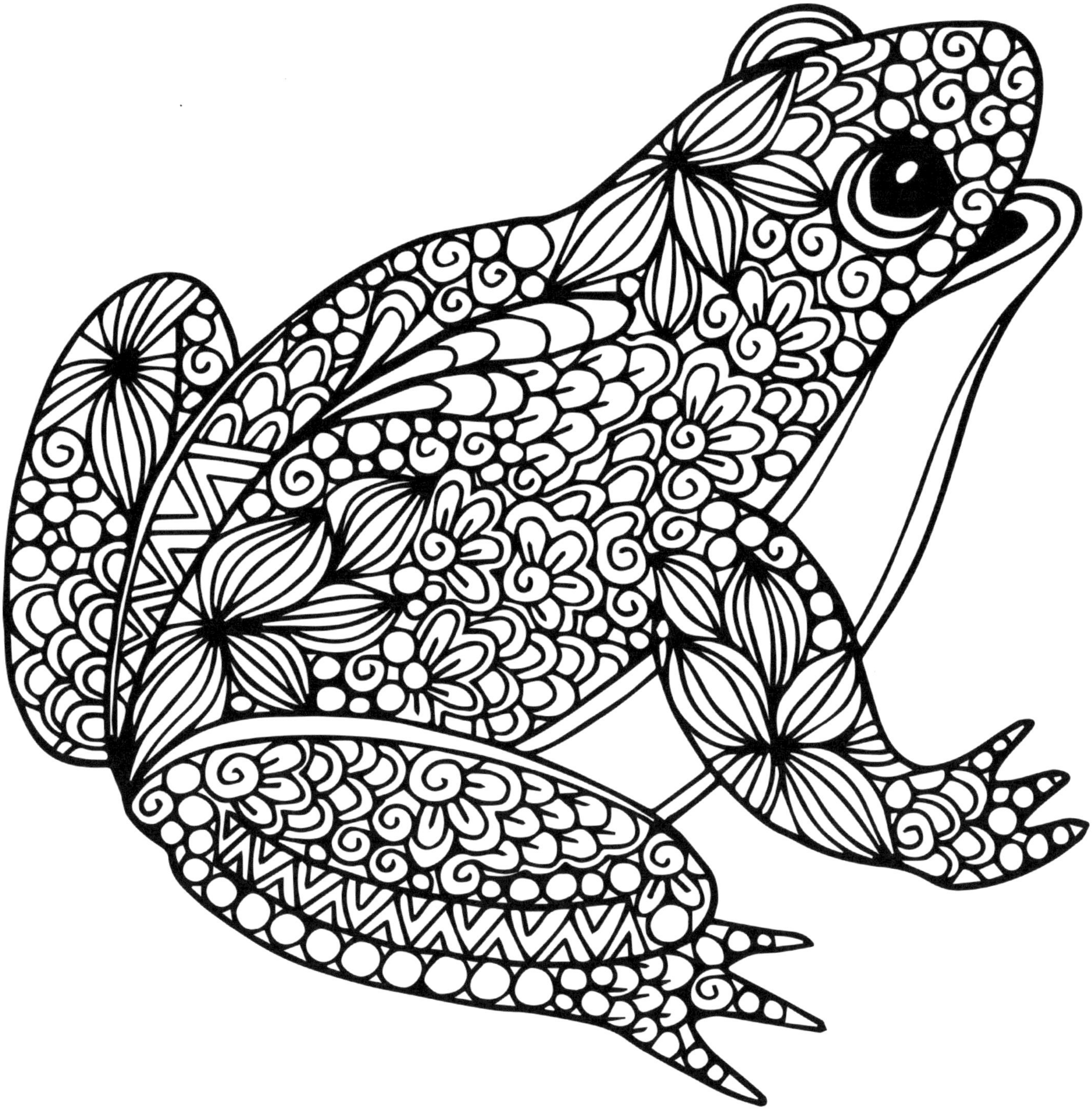

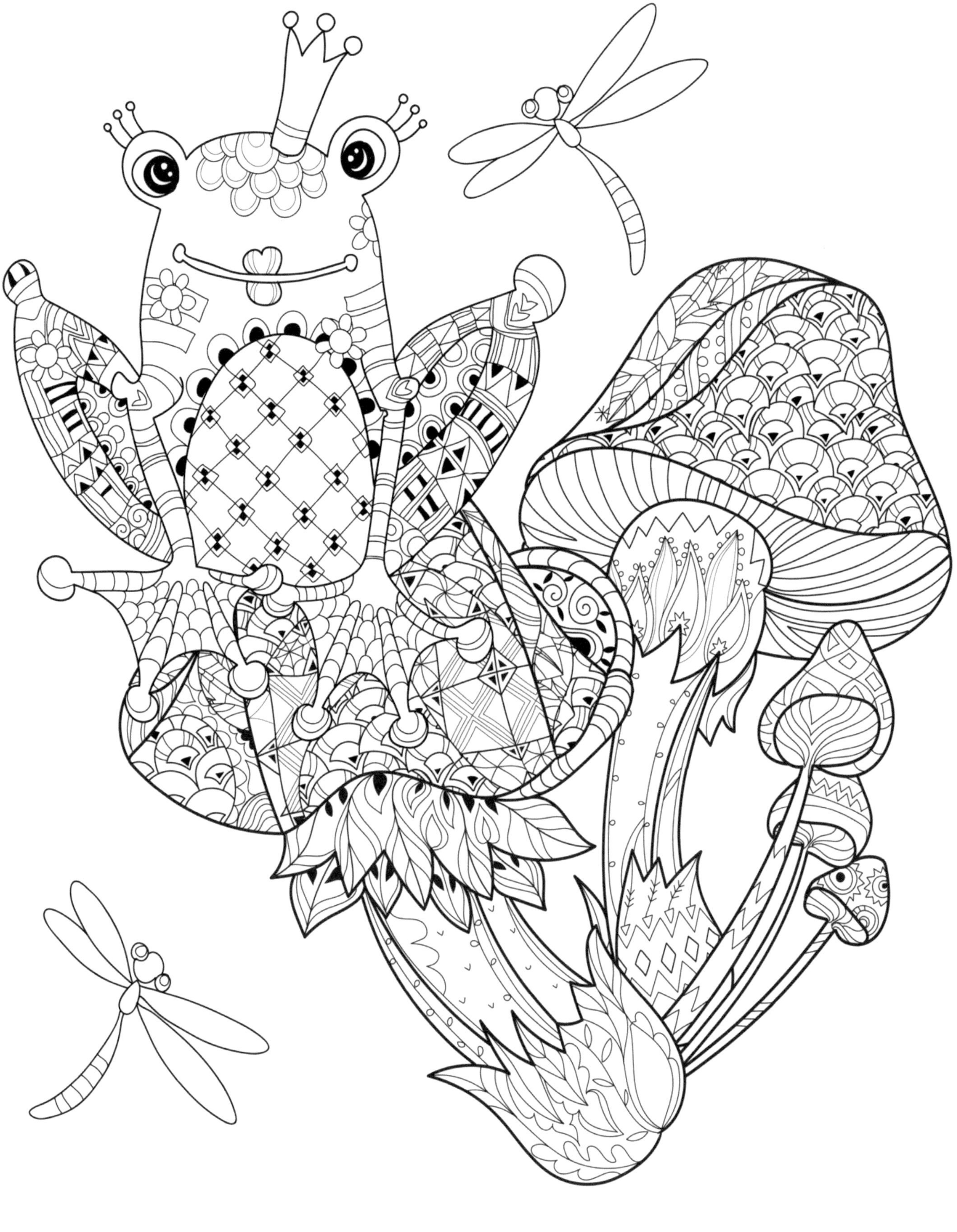

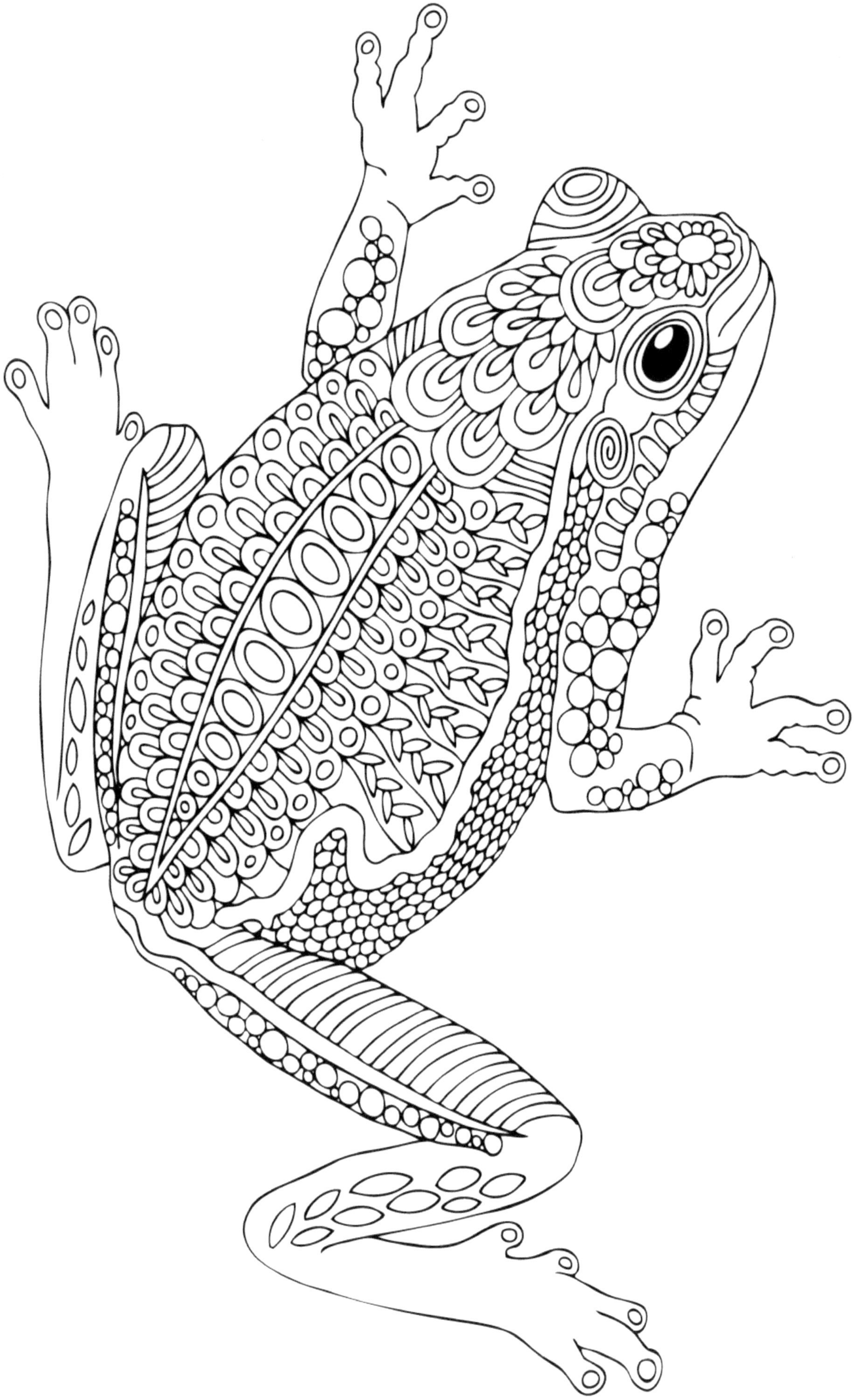

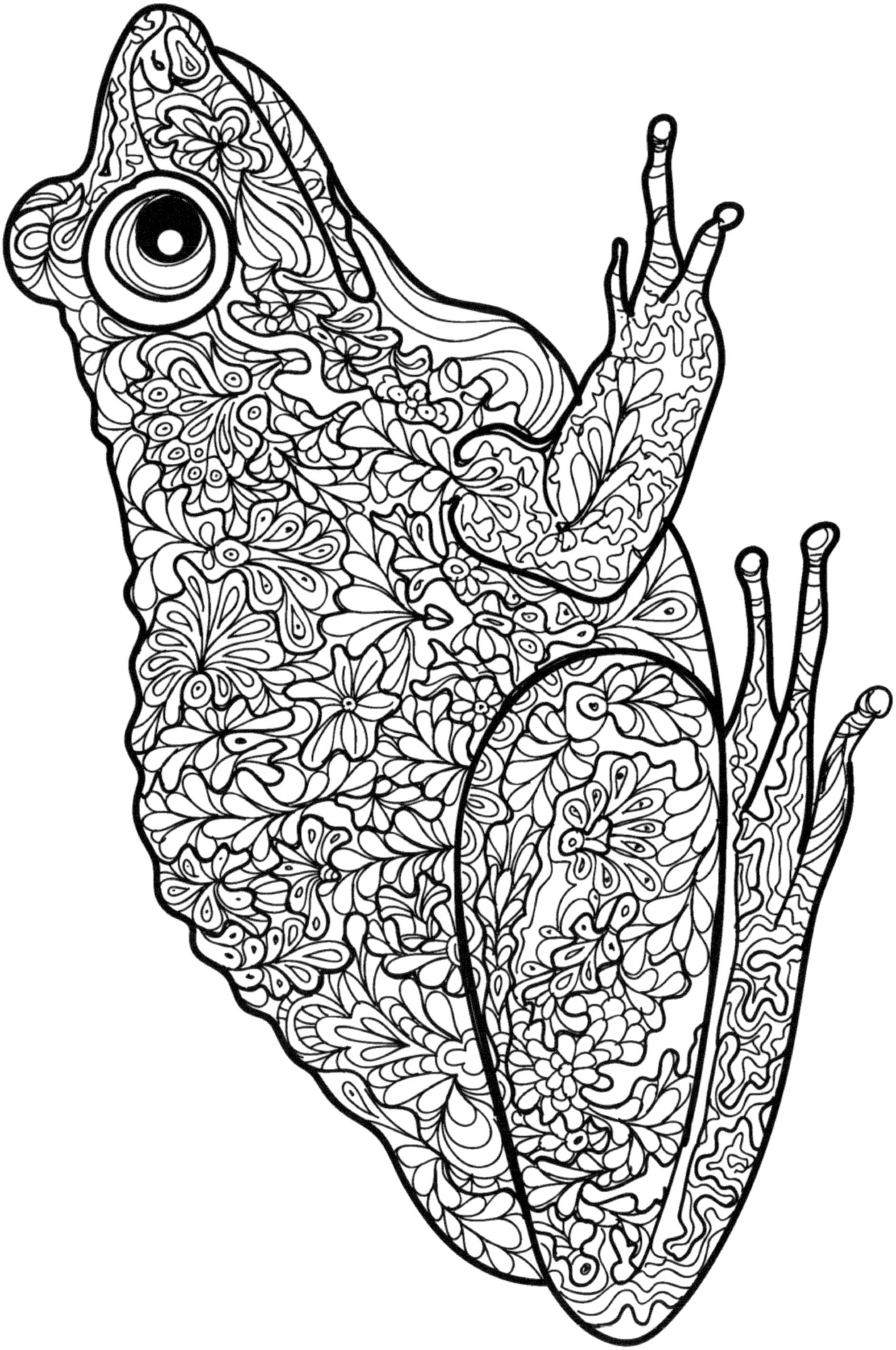

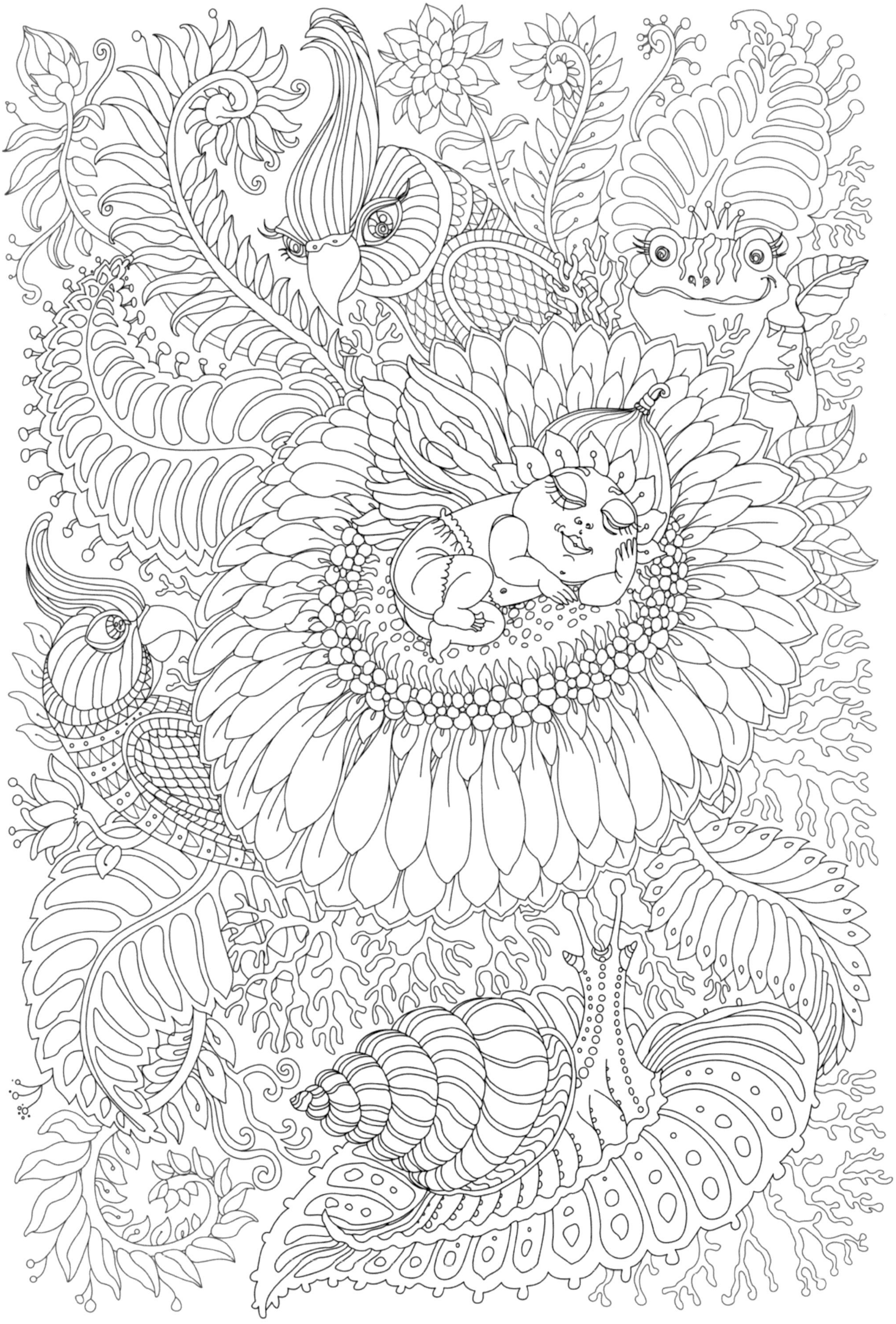

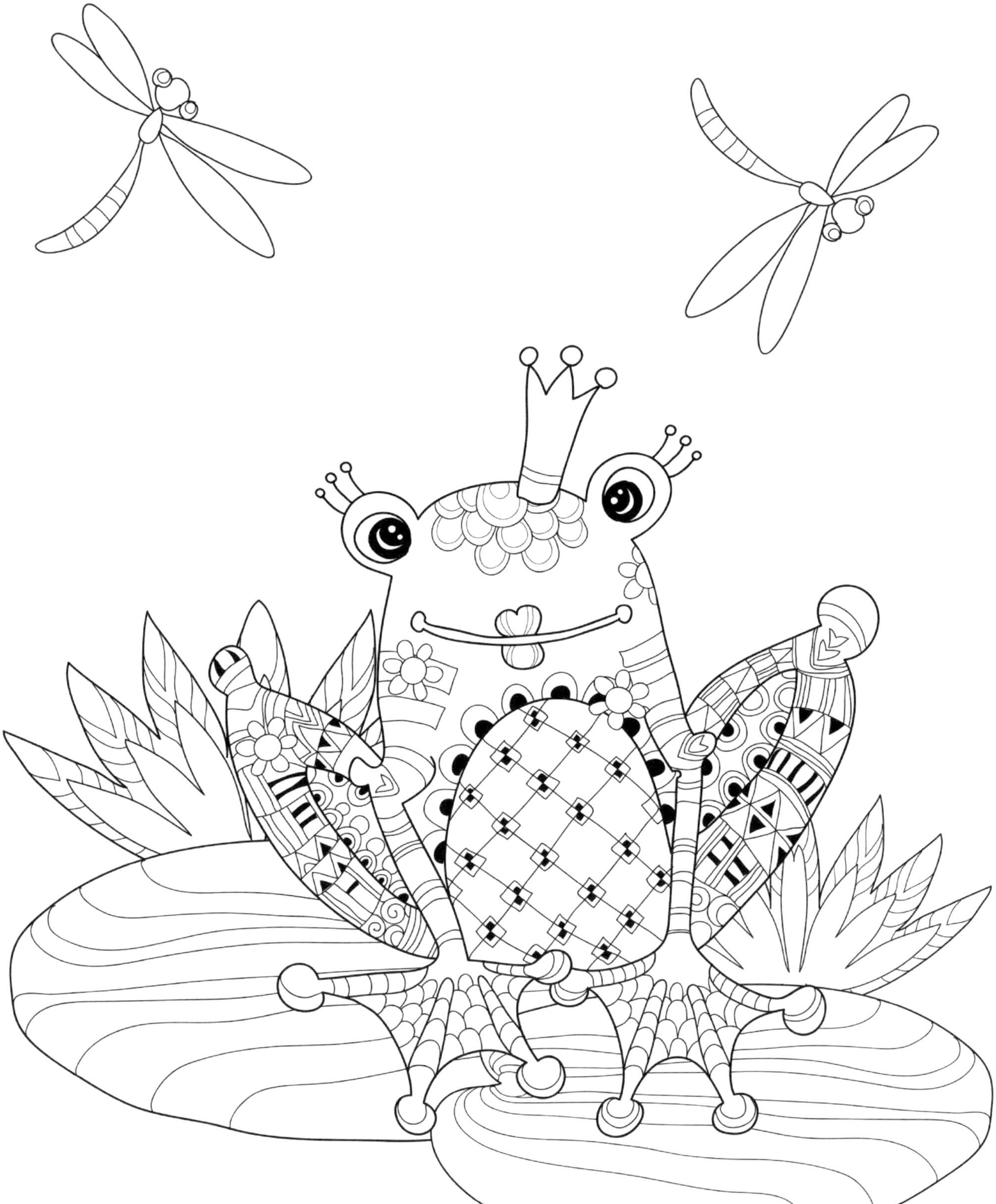

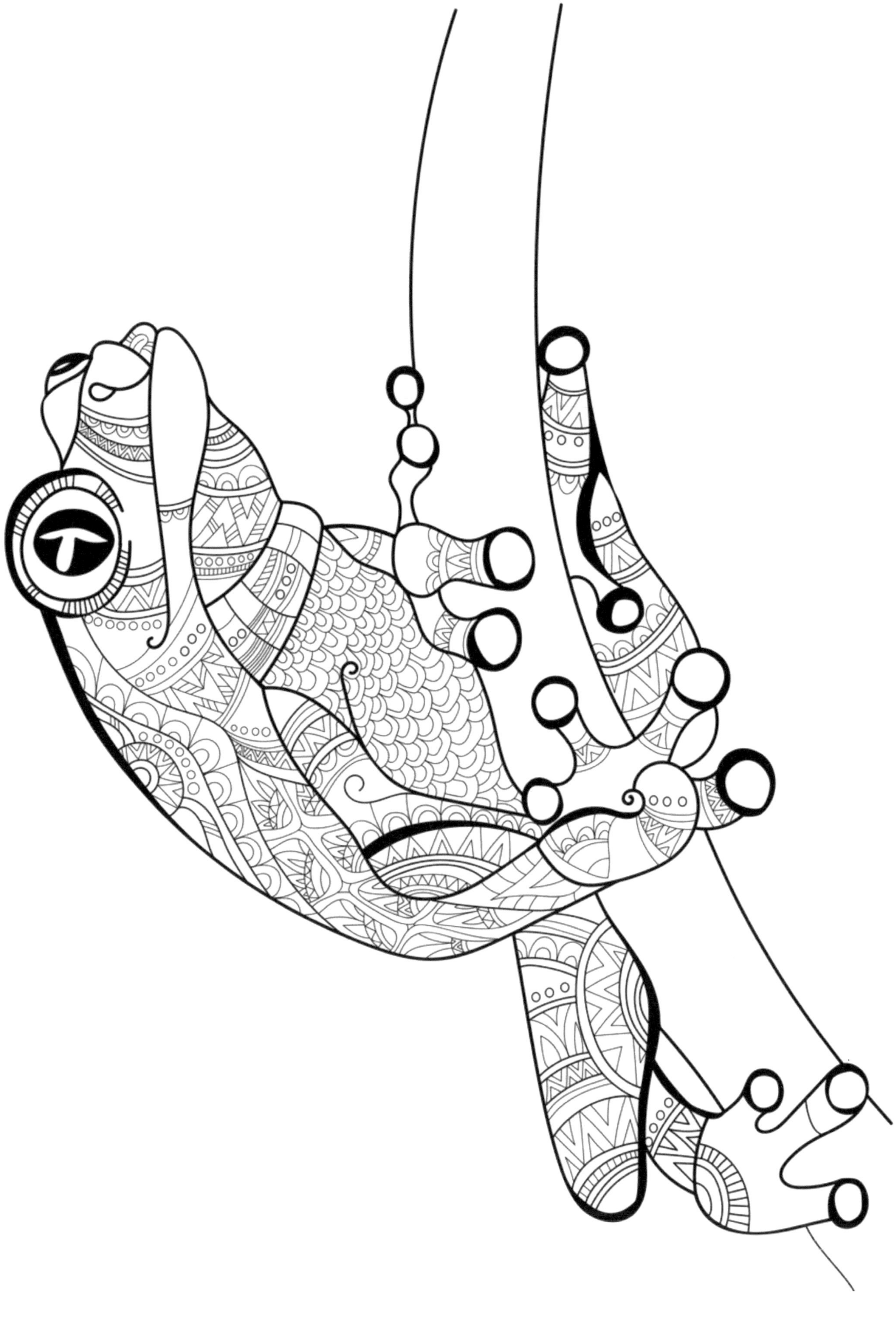

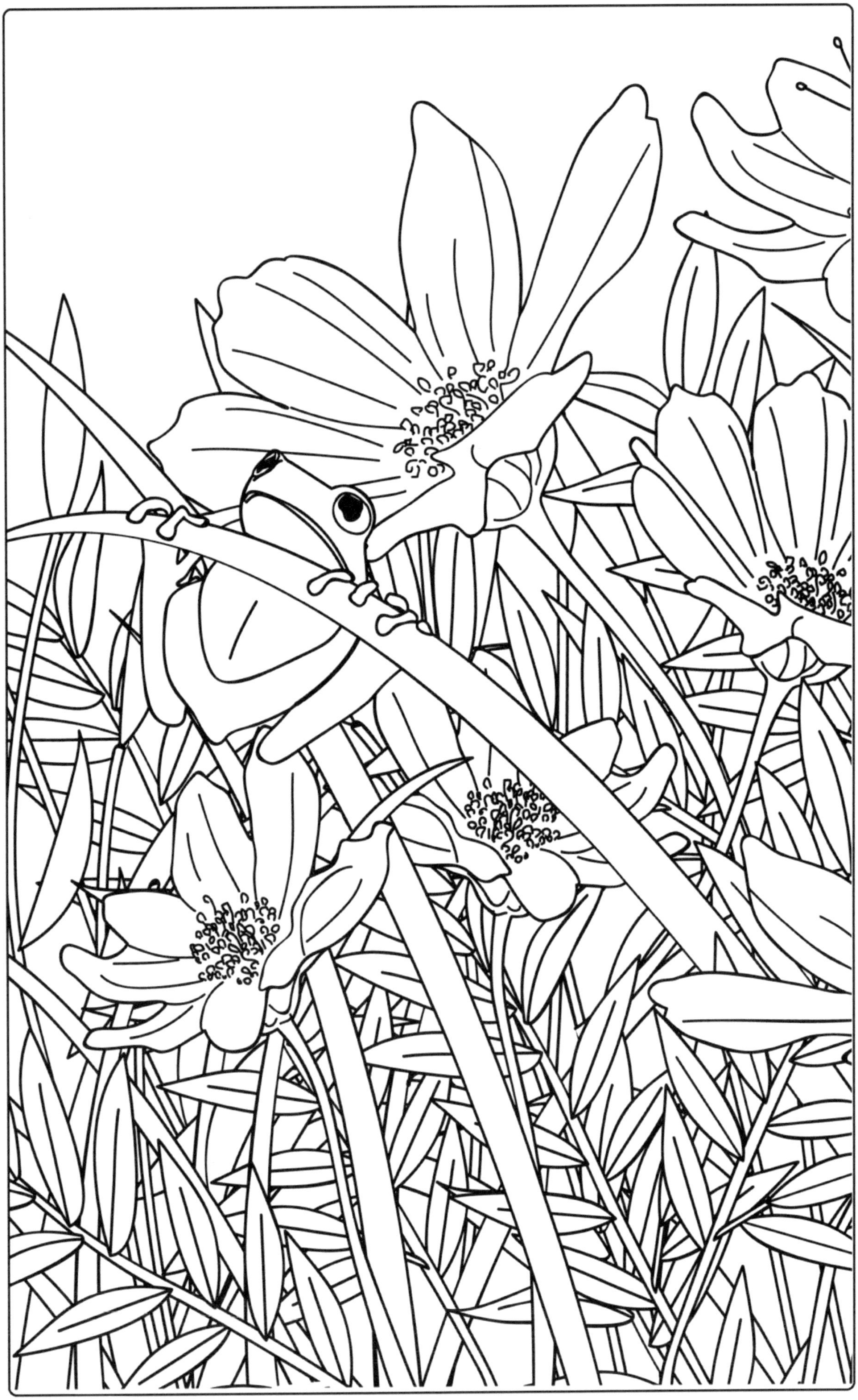

Thank you for coloring with us

Please rate & review

More Coloring Books For You at Amazon:

Rachel Mintz

Rainbow Wings
Butterflies Coloring Book

Nectar Birds

Hummingbirds
Coloring Book   Rachel Mintz

Adorable Giraffes
Coloring Book

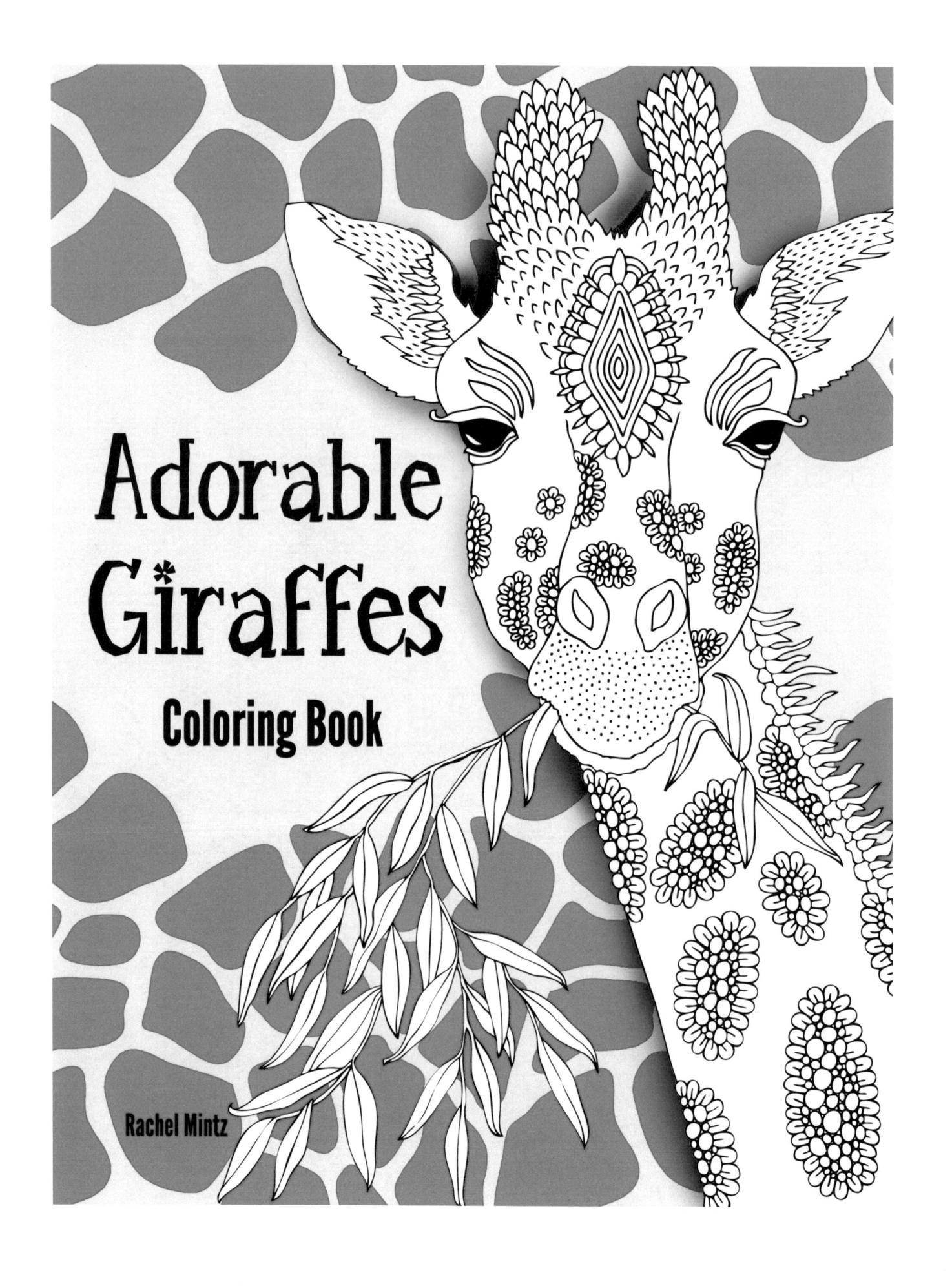

Rachel Mintz

Mighty Tigers
Coloring Book
Rachel Mintz

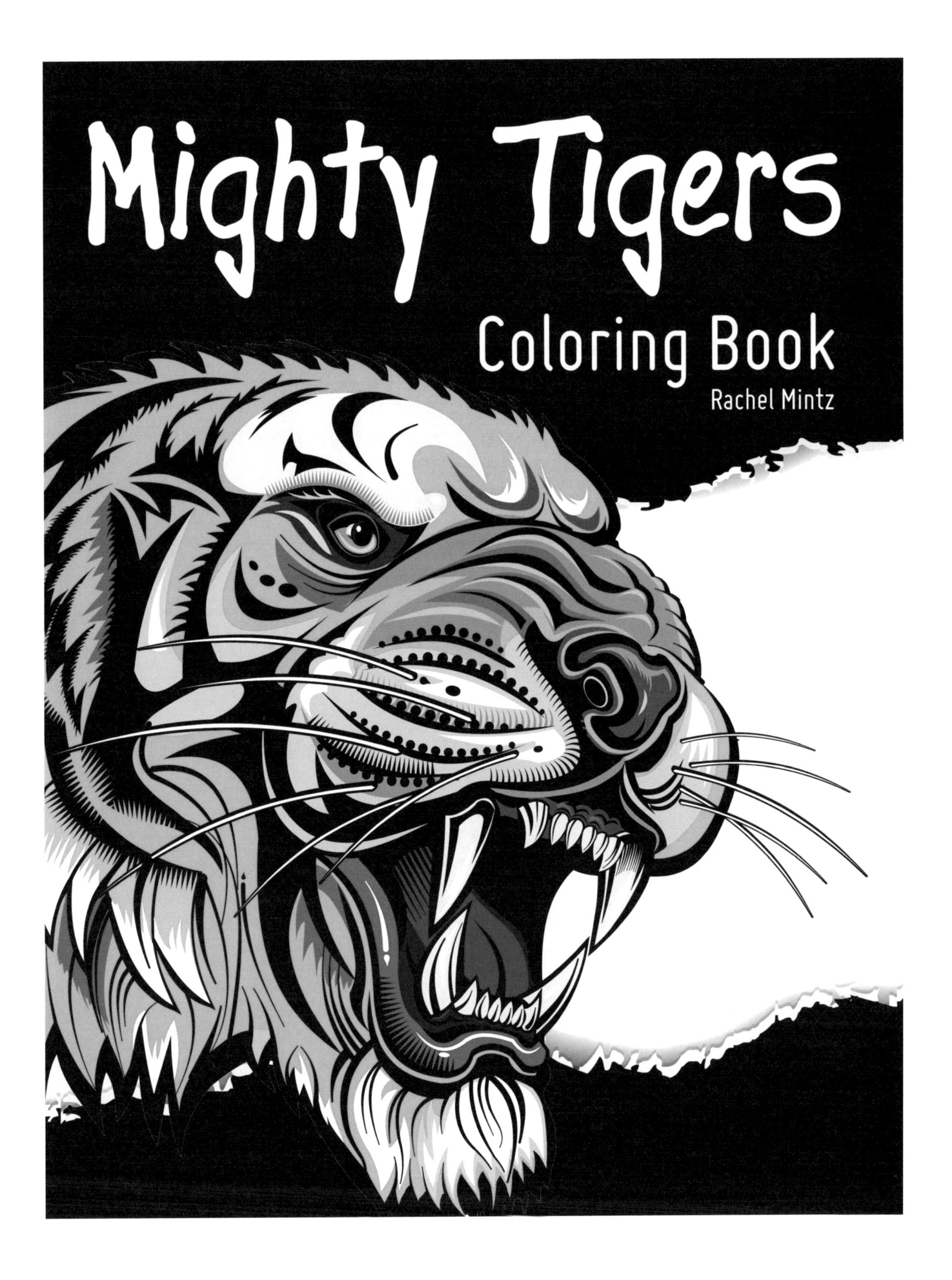

Join Our Coloring Books VIP Group
Members Get Giveaways, Deep Discount Offers,
Win Prizes – Visit Site To Join (It's Free)

www.ColoringBookHome.com

Thank you for coloring with us

Please rate & review

Manufactured by Amazon.ca
Bolton, ON